D1462297

Shakespeare's Birds

BY

PETER GOODFELLOW

ILLUSTRATED BY

PETER HAYMAN

THE OVERLOOK PRESS

WOODSTOCK, NEW YORK

Second printing in 1985 by
The Overlook Press, Lewis Hollow Road,
Woodstock, New York 12498

First published in Great Britain by Kestrel Books

ISBN: 0-87951-201-6
Library of Congress Catalog Card Number: 83-42982

Printed in Great Britain by Cambus Litho, East Kilbride

CONTENTS

'MELODIOUS BIRDS' *7*

SWAN *10*

WATER BIRDS *13*

BARNACLE GOOSE *20*

'WE'LL A-BIRDING TOGETHER' *24*

FALCONRY *27*

EAGLE *33*

OSPREY, KITE AND BUZZARD *36*

PARTRIDGE, PHEASANT AND QUAIL *40*

SNIPE, WOODCOCK AND LAPWING *42*

DOVE AND PIGEON *46*

CUCKOO AND HEDGE SPARROW *49*

OWL *53*

LARK *57*

HOUSE MARTIN *60*

ROBIN, WREN AND SWALLOW *62*

NIGHTINGALE *67*

BLACKBIRD, THRUSH AND STARLING *71*

ROOK, MAGPIE, JACKDAW, CHOUGH AND JAY *75*

RAVEN AND CARRION CROW *81*

SPARROW, FINCH, BUNTING AND WAGTAIL *86*

Suggestions for Further Reading *90*

Index of Birds *91*

Index of Shakespearian Sources *93*

Index of Plays and Poems *96*

Song Thrush

'MELODIOUS BIRDS'

Anyone who is fond of the countryside and country pursuits cannot fail to be impressed by Shakespeare's power to create vivid images which are clearly based on keen observation. He mentions over fifty birds in his writings, including such exotic species as peacock, vulture, ostrich, parrot, phoenix and turkey, and such vague names as finch, fowl and dove. However, it is the number of accurately observed British birds – which are the concern of this book and help to enliven his plays and poems – that is so impressive for a man who was not a naturalist but a poet and playwright. He observed birds with care and, when it came to writing about them later, often remembered details precisely.

Shakespeare lived in an age of inquiry. Serious naturalists were tussling with the problems of identifying and naming animals, birds and plants. *Avium Praecipuarum* by William Turner, the first printed bird book, was published in Latin in 1544, and John Kay of Cambridge published *De Rariorum Animalium* in 1570. James Fisher, the great modern historian of British birds, believed that by 1600 just one hundred and fifty species had been named on the British list. It was only after Shakespeare's death that the extensive travels and writings of Francis Willughby and John Ray greatly enlarged our knowledge of Britain's wildlife.

Stratford in Warwickshire was home for William Shakespeare until his teens. This flourishing market town, described by a contemporary as 'not inelegant', was set in a well-wooded valley, surrounded by fine farmland. Here, no doubt, his natural talent for observing the countryside was fostered. If, as is traditionally believed, he was later a schoolmaster in Gloucestershire, it may have been then that he gained his first-hand knowledge of the universally popular Elizabethan sport of hunting, to which there are so many references in his plays. There is also a tale that he was a poacher as a lad – he would surely have known the land and all that lived on it well in that case!

During his time as actor-manager-playwright in London his visits to Stratford were frequent and in 1597 he bought a grand house, New Place, with two gardens and two barns. By 1602 he employed a full-time gardener and had purchased another hundred and twenty acres of land. He was a countryman at heart; his wealth went back to the land.

His journey home from London – no doubt via Oxford – would have taken two days or so: plenty of time to observe rooks in the rookery, kites scavenging or skylarks singing. He did not settle down to enjoy his gardens at New Place until 1613, three years before he died, so all he knew of birds was learned from his boyhood excursions, his travels and any time spent on the estate of his friend, the Earl of Southampton. It may well be true to say that Shakespeare was no naturalist, and that he used some bird imagery repeatedly, as if fascinated by its poetic possibilities. But there can be no doubt that Shakespeare loved the countryside, as is shown, for example, in Tamora's words in *Titus Andronicus* when she says, 'The birds chant melody on every bush'. Shakespeare was attracted by 'melodious birds', and felt for the fowls which 'hear falcon's bells'. Above all, he leaves us with an impression of an observant and sensitive man, who loved his native Warwickshire, and could easily have sung the song he gave the Pages in *As You Like It*:

> *It was a lover and his lass,*
> > *With a hey, and a ho, and a hey nonino,*
> *That o'er the green corn-field did pass*
> > *In the spring time, the only pretty ring time,*
> > *When birds do sing, hey ding a ding, ding.*
> *Sweet lovers love the spring.*

SWAN

So doth the swan her downy cygnets save,
Keeping them prisoner underneath her wings.

— HENRY VI, PART I

For all the water in the ocean
Can never turn the swan's black legs to white ...

— TITUS ANDRONICUS

In the British Isles today, birdwatchers are accustomed to thinking of three species of swans – the whooper, Bewick's and the mute. But to millions who admire perhaps the most graceful of all our water birds, it is simply 'the swan' which graces our lakes and rivers – including the Avon, on which every year Stratford's thousands of visitors must see living reminders of the Bard. It was in 1623 that the swan was forever linked 'to the memory of my beloved, the author, Mr

William Shakespeare' in the lines Ben Jonson prefixed to the Folio edition:

Sweet Swan of Avon! What a sight it were
To see thee in our waters yet appear,
And make those flights upon the banks of Thames,
That so did take Eliza and our James!

These oft-quoted lines give Shakespeare a name associated with a royal bird, for by statute of Edward IV the swan was protected: 'None (but the King's son) shall have any Mark or Game of swans of his own, or to his use, except he have lands and tenements of Freehold worth five marks per annum ...'

So the name which Ben Jonson bestowed upon Shakespeare associated him with royalty. What honour could be greater than to be linked with the monarchs who had reigned during his lifetime? In addition, the epithet is charged with the beauty of the countryside he loved.

Shakespeare would have appreciated his friend's poetic imagery, for he often used the swan in his own verse. As with so many poets, Shakespeare conventionally repeats the ancient superstition that swans sing only before they die, using the idea particularly effectively in *Othello* when Emilia says, 'I will play the Swan, And die in music,' and then, dying, sings some of the plaintive old Willow Song. Although the 'swan song' is usually attributed to the mute swan, or 'tame swan' as it was called in Shakespeare's time, the wild, trumpeting cry of the migratory whooper swan has a better claim to be the bird from which the legend grew.

On the other hand, Imogen's metaphorical description of her homeland in *Cymbeline* is not at all conventional and suggests that somewhere Shakespeare had seen the bulky shape of a swan's nest by the shore of a large lake: a tiny island just offshore from a large continent:

> *I' the' world's volume*
> *Our Britain seems as of it, but not in't;*
> *In a great pool a swan's nest.*

The bird's large size and strikingly white plumage, its majestic grace on the water and its spectacular appearance in flight made it inevitable that man would bring the bird into his folklore, and that poets would extol it as a symbol of purity and virtue, as Shakespeare does in *The Rape of Lucrece*:

> *The crow may bathe his coal-black wings in mire*
> *And unperceiv'd fly with the filth away;*
> *But if the like the snow-white swan desire,*
> *The stain upon his silver down will stay.*

WATER BIRDS

... insatiate cormorant ...

Falstaff, during the ill-fated robbery on the road by Gadshill in *Henry IV, Part I*, declared that 'there's no more valour in that Poins than in a wild duck'. Certainly, ducks are easily scared and put to flight, but Poins was made of sterner stuff. 'Wild duck' may be a general term, but it is still a commonly accepted old name for the female *mallard*, or an alternative name for the species. I suspect Shakespeare well knew the difference and that Falstaff meant a *duck* not a *drake* because, in *Antony and Cleopatra*, Scarus talks to Enobarbus about Antony's actions at the Battle of Actium, saying:

> *The noble ruin of her magic, Antony,*
> *Claps on his sea-wing, and, like a doting mallard,*
> *Leaving the fight in height, flies after her.*

In March, especially over marshes and streams, many a *drake* mallard may be seen making courtship flights, closely following the *duck*.

Apart from the barnacle goose (see p.20), geese are not specifically identified by Shakespeare, although he does speak several times of 'wild geese'. Shortly before his death,

Macbeth refuses to believe reports of the enemy's advance and he curses his servant:

> *The devil damn thee black, thou cream-fac'd loon!*
> *Where got'st thou that goose look?*

Today we still say, 'You goose!' meaning 'You fool!' The goose is most likely one of the startled, white farmyard variety. Although 'loon' here means 'fool' and comes from a different root, the word was also used in the seventeenth century for the great northern diver, which is still called this in North America; a pun on the bird's name is very likely in this angry speech, especially when one realizes that a diver in summer plumage is black-faced and in winter, dirty white.

Shakespeare uses 'gull' to mean 'a fool, a dupe or a trick', or 'to fool'. The only time he wrote 'gull' and meant a bird was when a Senator in *Timon of Athens* ordered a servant to go to Timon to get the money he was owed:

*Peregrine Falcon
and Herons*

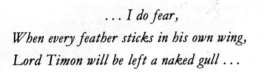

> *... I do fear,*
> *When every feather sticks in his own wing,*
> *Lord Timon will be left a naked gull ...*

This seems to mean that when every creditor has his proper due, Timon will be stripped. 'Gull' is used as a pun on 'dupe' and 'unfledged bird or chick', although the two senses of the word come from different roots.

Another odd word is found in Hamlet's much discussed statement, 'I know a hawk from a handsaw'. 'Handsaw' is sometimes emended to 'hernshaw', an old name for heron.

Kingfisher

Hawking at herons was a favourite sport. Hamlet is clearly saying, 'I can tell chalk from cheese!' Both 'hawk' and 'handsaw' are also names of tools. What a witty quibble this phrase is! Hamlet is not as mad as some of the characters in the play believe and he has certainly noticed that Rosencrantz and Guildenstern are bird of prey.

Shakespeare alludes to the kingfisher in *Henry VI, Part I* when Pucelle speaks of 'halcyon days'. The old Greek name for the kingfisher was 'halcyon', and it was thought that the kingfisher made a nest of fish-bones, floating it on the sea when all was calm. The belief was recorded by Pliny the Elder (A.D. 23–79) in his famous *Natural History*. Although Shakespeare uses the same poetic name in *King Lear*, he is

there alluding to an old English superstition. Kent, angry
with Oswald, says:

> *Such smiling rogues as these ...*
> *... turn their halcyon beaks*
> *With every gale and vary of their masters ...*

It was commonly believed that a dead kingfisher, hung by a
string, would always turn its bill to the wind. So, Oswald's
allegiance is as variable as the wind.

A rather unexpected bird appears in *Venus and Adonis*, where the teasing young man is described as

> *Like a dive-dapper peering through a wave,*
> *Who, being look'd on, ducks as quickly in.*

The bird is undoubtedly a grebe, which, when on the alert, swims with bill and head tilted up and body partly submerged, so that it really does look as if it is peering through a wave. Both the dabchick (or little grebe) and the great crested grebe have been called 'dive-dapper'. The former is commoner and probably always has been; the latter is more conspicuous but is confined to much larger lakes. Whichever Shakespeare meant – and the dabchick is more likely – it is an example of his keen observation.

The cormorant is a large, black and not particularly attractive bird, and is not well-known today except near its coastal breeding cliffs or on the wide estuaries where it feeds. It regularly visits inland waters in small numbers and has been

Dabchick

persecuted for years because it is supposed to deplete fish stocks. Its habit of bringing a large fish or eel to the surface before swallowing it has probably helped give it a bad name as a greedy bird. It used to be trained to catch fish; a string round its neck prevented it from swallowing those it caught, so it carried on fishing until its gullet was full. All of Shakespeare's uses of the name emphasize a greedy or devouring state of affairs: 'this cormorant war' in *Troilus and Cressida*; 'cormorant devouring Time' in *Love's Labour's Lost*; and a man's 'cormorant belly' in *Coriolanus*. The bird seems to have attracted Shakespeare's personal attention, because there was no strong literary tradition which would have tempted him to use it otherwise.

Cormorant

BARNACLE GOOSE

TRINCULO. *Monster, come, put some lime upon your fingers, and away with the rest.*

CALIBAN. *I will have none on't. We shall lose our time, And all be turned to barnacles, or to apes ...*

— THE TEMPEST

Poor Caliban! His new friends, Trinculo and Stephano, have given him a vision beyond his dreams. A monster, he has been Prospero's slave, but tipsy boastful Stephano promises that he can be a viceroy when he is King. However, Caliban fears that Prospero's magic will turn them into something dreadful.

Though it terrified Caliban, the barnacle goose is now thought by many to be the most attractive of the 'black geese'. It breeds in only three places in the world – the mountainous, inhospitable cliffs and rocky islands of Spitzbergen and Novaya Zemlya in the Arctic and in eastern Greenland. They often breed on wild crags more suited to eagles' eyries, safe from marauding Arctic foxes.

Shakespeare knew nothing of this – the nesting sites of the geese were unknown; their arrival in winter to parts of northern Britain and Ireland was part of a great mystery: where had they come from, where did they go? Black and white shellfish, sometimes washed ashore attached to rotten wood, were perhaps the key; for centuries imaginative men believed the incredible tale, perpetuated in *The Journal of Friar Odoric* written in 1330, that somewhere at sea the black and white shellfish miraculously hatched into the beautiful, pied geese.

It is not surprising that this myth does not appear anywhere in ancient Greek or Roman writings: today, practically all the world's population of barnacle geese winter in Scotland and Ireland; there is nothing to suggest that it has ever been any different. Our first certain knowledge of the goose comes from the early Middle Ages when we hear of Irish clergy who were permitted to eat the goose on feast days because of its being neither flesh nor born of flesh.

Barnacle Geese

Despite the arguments of some sceptics, this extraordinary piece of 'unnatural history' lived on. Shakespeare may well have seen a copy of John Gerard's *Herball* published in 1597, in which there was a woodcut showing geese hatching from a 'goose-tree' which Gerard claimed to have seen on an island off Lancashire.

Barnacle Geese

No wonder Caliban was afraid! The thought of being turned into a shellfish which became a bird which lived no one knew where was a dreadful one.

Furthermore, in this one sentence of imaginative brilliance Shakespeare devises a punishment which in its poetic imagery gives us echoes of the tempestuous island and the nature of Caliban – barnacles and apes.

'WE'LL A-BIRDING TOGETHER'

In Shakespeare's day the wealthy were very fond of country pursuits such as hunting, wild-fowling and falconry. Indeed, when Mr Page in *The Merry Wives of Windsor* offered an invitation to go 'a-birding together', he was probably suggesting the sort of expedition Shakespeare knew well. As a gentleman of means he was welcome at the country seats of the nobility, and his knowledge of birds probably came largely from outings like those planned by Mr Page. Guns, popularly known as 'birding pieces', were used. A well-observed wild-fowler at work is to be found in *A Midsummer Night's Dream*:

> *As wild geese that the creeping fowler eye,*
> *Or russet-pated choughs, many in sort,*
> *Rising and cawing at the gun's report,*
> *Sever themselves, and madly sweep the sky,*
> *So at his sight away his fellows fly . . .*

Other ways of catching birds in the sixteenth and seventeenth centuries were by using nets, springs and snares, traps and bird-lime. Shakespeare knew of them all. Sebastian in *The Tempest*, plotting the usurpation of the Duke, speaks of 'bat-fowling', which was the taking by night of birds which roost

24

in bushes. The birds were scared from the roost, attracted to lights carried by the hunters and caught in hand-held nets or on limed bushes. Other forms of nets were employed too, some baited with live, tethered birds which were to entice similar birds or birds of prey to the net; to these, Shakespeare compares the trapped Adonis: 'Look how a bird lies tangled in a net' (*Venus and Adonis*).

References to the woodcock tell us of other catching methods. The woodcock was considered stupid: it always walked the same paths or flew the same woodland rides, so

it was easy to catch. In *Hamlet*, both Polonius and Laertes refer to 'springes', used for catching woodcock. These were loops of fine string or hair, lying in the bird's path and attached delicately to a bowed hazel twig. When the bird trod in the loop, its leg was caught, a trigger was released and the bent twig whipped up, dangling the helpless bird. They were also caught in snares, and even in the ugly-jawed gin-trap which had probably been set for bigger prey – 'so strives the woodcock with the gin', says Lord Clifford when the Duke of York is captured (*Henry VI, Part III*).

Shakespeare mentions bird-liming more than any other form of bird-catching. It appears three times in *Henry VI, Part II* alone. Bird-lime was a sticky substance made, for example, from the bark of the holly and spread on twiggy boughs of trees such as birch, willow or aspen. Any bird touching the lime became stuck, fluttered and became more entangled. Shakespeare uses the substance metaphorically to describe someone who has been ensnared, as when Ursula says in *Much Ado About Nothing*, 'She's lim'd, I warrant you; we have caught her' or when Malvolio, full of pride after he has received the counterfeit letter, says of his mistress Olivia, 'I have lim'd her' (*Twelfth Night*).

FALCONRY

Peregrine Falcon

O for a falc'ner's voice,
To lure this tassel-gentle back again!

— ROMEO AND JULIET

Hillo, ho, ho, boy! Come, bird, come.

— HAMLET

Falconry has been known for over three thousand years, spreading from its ancient origins in the East. By the ninth century falconry – the word is synonymous with 'hawking' – had arrived in Britain. As the years passed, its role changed from a method of hunting food to a leisure-time activity. By the reigns of Elizabeth I and James I it was very popular

27

among all those who had time and money to practise the sport. Indeed, so much love and care, time and money, is poured into bringing the bird to perfection that falconry has long been thought of as more of an art than a sport.

Every falcon was taught to know the falconer's voice, as Juliet and Hamlet well knew. Most people must have understood a great deal about the art – it was full of excitement and glamour, and there were many retainers who could pass on the technicalities of the sport to the groundlings. Did Shakespeare own his own hawk? As a gentleman, with his own coat-of-arms, he would have been entitled to fly a goshawk. He knew so much about the sport that he *must* have been personally involved, perhaps on visits to one of his noble friends; only an expert could so naturally and accurately use so many technical terms; and only an informed audience could grasp the significance of a multitude of allusions. For example, Juliet's poignant cry, 'Hist! Romeo, hist! – O for a falc'ner's voice, To lure this tassel-gentle back again' is the more desperate when one realizes that a 'tassel-gentle' is a male peregrine falcon, a prince's bird, a bird of great price and spectacular courage, which would be a great loss to any falconer. As great a loss was Romeo to Juliet. The falcon (the female peregrine) is better able to pursue 'the ducks i' the river', as Pandarus says to Troilus and Cressida. Interestingly, the peregrine is still called the duck hawk in North America.

Shakespeare has documented his knowledge of the hunt very thoroughly in *Henry VI, Part II*:

KING.   *But what a* point, *my lord, your falcon made,*
           And what a pitch *she flew above the rest!*
           To see how God in all His creatures works!
           Yea, man and birds are fain of climbing high.
SUFFOLK.   *No marvel, an it like your Majesty,*
           My Lord Protector's hawks do tow'r *so well;*
           They know their master loves to be aloft,
           And bears his thoughts above his falcon's pitch.
GLOUCESTER. *My lord, 'tis but a base ignoble mind*
           That mounts no higher than a bird can soar.

'Point' is the hovering over the spot where prey has been seen; 'pitch' is the height to which the bird rises before swooping; 'tower' is spiralling to a height; and 'soar' describes the wide sweeps a hawk makes on outstretched wings.

Even if Shakespeare did not have his own hawk, he must have been very familiar with the lengthy and painful process of 'manning' a hawk, which means making it familiar with its keeper. In *The Taming of the Shrew* Katherine, Kate the Curst, as wild as the wildest hawk, with claws as sharp, meets her match in Petruchio who says:

My falcon now is sharp *and passing empty,*
And till she stoop *she must not be* full-gorg'd,
For then she never looks upon her lure.
Another way I have to man *my* haggard,
To make her come, and know her keeper's call,
That is, to watch her, as we watch these kites
That bate, *and beat, and will not be obedient.*

Only a fully trained hawk would be able to 'stoop' – that is, dive on to some quarry. Until then it is kept hungry ('sharp'), kept chasing the 'lure' (a piece of wood or leather with a small morsel of meat attached, tied to a length of leather); repeatedly it tries to fly off its perch to which it is tied by 'jesses'; the jesses restrain it and it 'bates', dangling, flapping madly. The most difficult bird to train is a 'haggard', a wild-caught, mature hawk; a young hawk taken from a nest is much more amenable. What a haggard Kate proved to be! But what dreadful irony is in the same word when Othello says of Desdemona:

> *If I do prove her* haggard,
> *Though that her* jesses *were my dear heart-strings,*
> *I'd whistle her off and let her down the wind*
> *To prey at fortune.*

A falconer who let his bird fly off downwind was almost sure to lose it.

Peregrine Falcon

One of Shakespeare's best hawking images is found in Tranio's description of Bianca in *The Taming of the Shrew*:

> *Master, your love must live a maid at home;*
> *And therefore has he closely* mew'd *her up,*
> *Because she will not be annoy'd with suitors.*

'Mew' or 'enmew' means to 'enclose' or 'shut up'. It comes from an old French word meaning 'a bird's time of moult'. Later it meant the place where hawks or falcons were kept to moult. What a lovely idea it is that Shakespeare mews up Bianca, whose suitors find her anyway, and that at the end of the period of manning the only well-trained falcon is Kate!

Although there are many references to hawking and falconry in Shakespeare's plays and poems, he names only two other species besides the peregrine. In *Twelfth Night*, Sir Toby and company plan to trick Malvolio; Maria drops a forged love letter where he is likely to pass by, and the practical jokers watch.

FABIAN.   *What dish of poison has she dressed him!*
SIR TOBY. *And with what wing the* staniel checks *at it!*

'Staniel' was a common Elizabethan name for the kestrel; 'checks' is a falconer's term meaning 'hovers'. The kestrel is far and away the most able British bird at hovering. What a lively description of Malvolio who, as the knave and kestrel, hovers over each word in the letter!

Secondly, an old name for the sparrow hawk was musquet hawk (from the old French 'mousquet' or 'mouchet', from 'mouche', a fly, an allusion to its small size), and we find this name used once by Shakespeare in *The Merry Wives of Windsor*: 'How now, my eyas-musket, what news with you?' An eyas was a nestling falcon or hawk. Mistress Ford seems to be describing Falstaff's page as a 'bright little chap'.

The plays are full of precise references to hawks and falcons, and everywhere they add sharply to the drama. In *Devon Birds* in May 1976 R.W. Hayman recorded the extraordinary sight of *a barn owl bringing down a kestrel* (which was diving repeatedly at it). Strange though this event was, it is not without precedent, as we hear in *Macbeth*:

> *'Tis unnatural,*
> *Even like the deed that's done. On Tuesday last,*
> *A falcon, tow'ring in her pride of place,*
> *Was by a mousing owl hawk'd at and kill'd.*

Shakespeare had seen it happen too.

EAGLE

I saw Jove's bird, the Roman eagle ...

— CYMBELINE

...an eagle, madam,
Hath not so green, so quick, so fair an eye
As Paris hath.

— ROMEO AND JULIET

Yet looks he like a king. Behold, his eye,
As bright as is the eagle's, lightens forth
Controlling majesty ...

— RICHARD II

For centuries Man has looked in awe and wonder at eagles. In every part of the world the power of the eagle is still thought to be magical. This large majestic bird is near the top of the food-pyramid. It preys on others who prey on others, but nothing, except man, hunts the eagle. He is king.

Our traditional eagle is full of courage and strength. 'God delivered his people out of Egypt and bore them upon eagles' wings'. Thus the Bible, together with classical authors and mediaeval compilers of encyclopedias, gave birth to a literary tradition which resulted in 'the princely eagle' on the Elizabethan stage. Shakespeare mentions the bird in every royal play – but not the tragedies of *King Lear* and *Hamlet*. He uses the word 'eagle' many times but never names a particular

Golden Eagle

species. In Europe, tales of eagles' power and grandeur have probably grown up from observations of the golden eagle. With this bird Shakespeare firmly follows tradition. Richard of Gloucester in *Richard III* arranges Clarence's arrest and loyal Hastings declares:

> *More pity that the eagle should be mew'd*
> *Whiles kites and buzzards prey at liberty.*

This fine comparison strikingly emphasizes Clarence's imprisoned royalty compared with the scavengers' freedom.

Imperial power is very interestingly described in *Titus Andronicus*:

> *The eagle suffers little birds to sing,*
> *And is not careful what they mean thereby,*
> *Knowing that with the shadow of his wings*
> *He can at pleasure stint their melody . . .*

Kites and Ravens

Although the eagle is so often associated with royalty and auspicious occasions, it is easy to understand how early man could believe that if an eagle's presence was lucky, its departure was unlucky. Cassius certainly felt this before the battle of Philippi, as recorded in *Julius Caesar*:

> *Coming from Sardis, on our former ensign*
> *Two mighty eagles fell; and there they perch'd,*
> *Gorging and feeding from our soldiers' hands,*
> *Who to Philippi here consorted us.*
> *This morning are they fled away and gone,*
> *And in their steads do ravens, crows, and kites,*
> *Fly o'er our heads, and downward look on us*
> *As we are sickly prey.*

How truly the birds foretold the battle's outcome.

OSPREY, KITE AND BUZZARD

Well ta'en, and like a buzzard.

— THE TAMING OF THE SHREW

Detested kite!

— KING LEAR

Of all families of birds today, the birds of prey are, perhaps, the most studied, most written about and most precious. In recent years, because of pesticides, many populations of them have suffered all over the world. Today, birdwatchers go miles to see migrant hawks and rare breeding species: to Hawk Mountain, Pennsylvania; to Falsterbo, Sweden; and to Loch Garten, Scotland.

But two of the three species here considered, the buzzard and the kite, were poorly thought of by Shakespeare and his contemporaries. Only the osprey, like the falcon and the eagle, was admired, as a quotation from *Coriolanus* indicates:

I think he'll be to Rome
As is the osprey to the fish, who takes it
By sovereignty of nature.

Turner, in his work of 1544, wrote that 'the Osprey is a bird much better known today to Englishmen than many who keep fish in stews would wish'. It is very likely that Shakespeare knew that. The osprey still raids fish-ponds (stews) and fish-hatcheries.

In the first scene of *Cymbeline* we learn that Imogen, the king's daughter, has married 'a poor but worthy gentleman'. Cymbeline is enraged; but Imogen defends herself, unsuccessfully:

IMOGEN.   *I chose an eagle,*
          And did avoid a puttock.
CYMBELINE. *Thou took'st a beggar . . .*

In the sixteenth century the 'puttock' was the bird we now call the red kite. In *Henry VI, Part II* King Henry and Queen Margaret discover the murdered body of the Duke of Gloucester, and Warwick says:

WARWICK. *Who finds the partridge in the puttock's nest*
          But may imagine how the bird was dead,
          Although the kite soar with unbloodied beak?
          Even so suspicious is this tragedy.
MARGARET.   *. . . Is Beaufort termed a kite? Where are his talons?*

What good fortune the kite had another name! Shakespeare was able to name the bird three times in six lines without any irritating repetition and put a spitting alliteration on the lips of Warwick. Thersites, in *Troilus and Cressida*, also uses the bird as an image of contempt when he says, 'To be . . . an owl, a puttock, or a herring without roe, I would not care'.

37

The kite is often mentioned elsewhere, nearly always in association with death, as when York in *Henry VI, Part II* says:

> *The deadly-handed Clifford slew my steed;*
> *But match to match I have encount'red him,*
> *And made a prey for carrion kites and crows*
> *Even of the bonny beast he lov'd so well.*

Modern hygiene has cleaned up our towns so effectively that, in Great Britain, only a few pairs of these scavengers are left in wooded valleys in mid-Wales. In Shakespeare's time, however, kites were well-known within the city 'so that the very gardens and courts, or yards of houses are not secure from

Kite

Buzzards

their ravine. For which cause our good housewives are very angry with them, and of all birds hate and curse them most' (Willughby). The rogue Autolycus in *The Winter's Tale* records another characteristic of the kite: 'My traffic is sheets; when the kite builds, look to lesser linen.' Bird books today still record the kite's partiality for lining its nest with rags. This lively comment vividly describes the scrounging villain just before he picks the clown's pocket.

To a falconer, the goshawk was a fine hunter, whereas the buzzard – another hawk – was considered a foolish, sluggish bird. This is interestingly shown in Petruchio's and Katherine's conversation about marriage in *The Taming of the Shrew*, which is full of puns and venom:

KATHERINA.   *Well ta'en and like a buzzard.*
PETRUCHIO.   *O, slow-wing'd turtle, shall a buzzard take thee?*

It is a great shame that this large, brown hawk, whose graceful circling in the sky appeals to so many people today, was so unpopular in the seventeenth century.

PARTRIDGE, PHEASANT AND QUAIL

... his quails ever beat mine ...
— ANTONY AND CLEOPATRA
... there's a partridge wing saved ...
— MUCH ADO ABOUT NOTHING

What a surprise that these popular game birds do not appear on the menu in the feasts in *The Taming of the Shrew* or *Timon of Athens*! They have enjoyed changing fortunes over the centuries. The partridge was widespread in Shakespeare's time, but its numbers today are lower. The diminutive quail was probably common in Britain until the end of the eighteenth century but is now rare enough to be afforded special protection by the Protection of Birds Act. The pheasant, however, was but fairly well established in England by the late sixteenth century (after its introduction by the Normans), and so was, no doubt, less often seen by Shakespeare than by us.

When Beatrice, in *Much Ado About Nothing*, is at the masked ball, she talks unwittingly to the disguised Benedick about himself. She says that when Benedick hears what she has to say about him he is sure to be struck 'into melancholy; and then there's a partridge wing saved, for the fool will eat no supper that night'.

Not only was the bird considered a delicacy, but so were quail and pheasant. The quail was much enjoyed at the table by people right across Europe. Elaborate snaring devices made of nets were set up and quails were lured to them by a hunter blowing on a quail-pipe which imitated the birds' distinctive calls.

The first place among birds at the table was assigned to the pheasant. How highly it was prized is delightfully hinted at in *The Winter's Tale*. When Autolycus is teasing the shepherd into believing he is a courtier, the following strange conversation ensues:

SHEPHERD. *My business, sir, is to the King.*
AUTOLYCUS. *What advocate hast thou to him?*
SHEPHERD. *I know not, an't like you.*
CLOWN. *Advocate's the court-word for a pheasant; say you have none.*
SHEPHERD. *None, sir; I have no pheasant, cock nor hen.*

The clown confuses the two kinds of 'court', and clearly has in mind the common practice in Shakespeare's day of bribing the judge with a bird; a pheasant would have been specially welcome!

SNIPE, WOODCOCK AND LAPWING

... to seem the lapwing ...

— MEASURE FOR MEASURE

Shall I not find a woodcock too?

— MUCH ADO ABOUT NOTHING

These three birds have all provided gourmets with food for centuries. In Shakespeare's time snipe's flesh was considered tender, sweet and 'of an excellent rellish'; the taste of woodcock, especially its leg, was held in high esteem; and lapwing's eggs were a delicacy. How strange it is then that Shakespeare uses the names contemptuously. In *Othello*, after Iago has stirred up Roderigo, he says of him:

> *... I mine own gain'd knowledge should profane*
> *If I would time expend with such a snipe*
> *But for my sport and profit.*

And Grumio in *The Taming of the Shrew*, referring to Lucentio disguised as a schoolmaster, says, 'O this woodcock, what an ass it is!' Both birds' names clearly mean 'fool'. The reason is clear with 'woodcock', because, as we have seen, that

Lapwings and Snipe in flight
Lapwings and Woodcock below

species was the easiest game-bird to catch in a net or snare and so was described as a foolish or simple creature. But why was it insulting to be called a snipe? Two answers are possible. Firstly, because a snipe looks an odd, ungainly, ill-fashioned bird with its very long bill, it is natural that over the years men have been called 'snipe-faced' and 'snipe-nosed' and, perhaps, by contraction, simply 'snipe'. Secondly, snipe live in muddy, messy, damp places – often called 'snipe-bogs'. Only a fool or unsavoury character (a gutter-snipe) would be found in such an uncomfortable place. There is also the suggestion that Iago is just playing the sportsman and that Roderigo is a fool of a man to allow himself to become the game-bird.

The snipe reference is unique, but Shakespeare was very fond of imagery which used the woodcock. One of the most amusing examples is in *Love's Labour's Lost* when Birowne, hidden up a tree, looks down at the men smitten by Cupid and says to himself, 'Four woodcocks in a dish!'; by so doing he sets going a train of thought which mixes together the foolishness and tasty desirability of infatuation! The most tragic references to this bird are in *Hamlet*. When Polonius finds out that Hamlet loves Ophelia, she defends his over-tures of love, saying that Hamlet had 'given countenance to his speech . . . With almost all the holy vows of heaven'. But Polonius tetchily describes these as 'springes to catch wood-cocks', implying that Hamlet was just offering smiling deceits to catch the foolish and unwary. With dreadful irony in the last scene, it is Ophelia's brother, Laertes, who is

44

trapped. Wounded deeply by Hamlet, he falls and is tended by Osric, who asks, 'How is't, Laertes?' He replies, 'Why, as a woodcock, to my own springe, Osric'.

It is pleasing to record that the beautiful lapwing is given a better deal by Shakespeare. Laertes's second, Osric, is described by Horatio as 'this lapwing [which] runs away with the shell on his head'. This is an amusing picture of the lad, who looks as young as a lapwing chick which has just hatched and is able to run almost as soon as it is out of the egg – with, as tradition would have it, its shell on its head.

In *Measure for Measure* Lucio, the eccentric dandy, goes to Isabella to ask her to help her brother. In the conversation he admits that ''tis my familiar sin With maids to seem the lapwing'. Shakespeare must have seen the cock lapwing's showy mating display to have penned such a picture. The lapwing's movements must have fascinated Shakespeare, as we see from *Much Ado About Nothing*:

> *For look where Beatrice, like a lapwing, runs*
> *Close by the ground . . .*

'Lapwing', from two Anglo-Saxon words, seems to mean 'twisting as it runs' and has nothing to do with wings and flying. It is a perfect word to describe Beatrice. Finally, Adriana in *The Comedy of Errors* says, 'Far from her nest the lapwing cries', which sadly describes her own state, being away from her love. The lapwing *does* call distractedly when disturbed from its nest – but only when it is some distance away, so that predators will not harm the eggs.

DOVE AND PIGEON

Turtle Dove

... as gently as any sucking dove ...
— A MIDSUMMER NIGHT'S DREAM

Many an estate and farm had a dovecote in Shakespeare's time, just like the one that Juliet's nurse sat beneath. The birds looked attractive, cooed gently and romantically – and provided the landowner with a plentiful supply of fresh meat; many potions and medicines were concocted from their flesh and blood, to cure dim sight, colic, gout and falling hair; their droppings were used as fertilizer, and young doves were eaten as delicacies. So it is not surprising that old Gobbo, in *The Merchant of Venice*, offers Bassanio 'a dish of doves'.

The dove has long been associated with gentleness, love and faithfulness. In ancient Greece the dove was one of Aphrodite's birds, a tradition Shakespeare acknowledges in *Venus and Adonis*, in which Venus says, 'Two strengthless doves will draw me through the sky'.

Shakespeare is not so fond of the name 'pigeon', and nowhere does he make a clear reference to the wild wood pigeon, the common pigeon of our woods and stubble fields. Pigeons and doves feed their young on regurgitated food, partially digested, which is called 'pigeon's milk'. The adult pumps this directly into the young's throat, both birds on the nest, bill to bill, for several minutes. This earnest, close-contact behaviour is amusingly used by Shakespeare in *As You Like It* when Celia and Rosalind are talking together:

Turtle Doves, domestic doves

CELIA.   *Here comes Monsieur Le Beau.*

ROSALIND. *With his mouth full of news.*

CELIA.   *Which he will put on us as pigeons feed their young.*

ROSALIND. *Then shall we be news-cramm'd.*

Shakespeare *does* refer several times to one particular species – the turtle dove. Shakespeare, in common with many others, usually called it simply the 'turtle' – no relation of the reptile, but derived from the French *tourterelle*, from the Latin *turtur*, which is an imitation of the bird's call.

This beautiful dove, with rufous back and wings, pink breast, set off with a black and white tail, is a summer migrant, heralding its arrival with its purring song. A large part of its diet is made up of the seeds of the weed fumitory; we can well imagine Shakespeare saw them on the stubble fields feeding on 'rank fumiter and furrow-weeds' (*King Lear*). It was the symbol of constancy; the lover as true 'as turtle to her mate' (*Troilus and Cressida*) was rare indeed.

A very lively mention of the birds is in *The Merry Wives of Windsor*. Mistress Ford and Mistress Page are determined to get the better of Falstaff: 'we'll teach him to know turtles from jays'. On the face of it, these two birds are alike – pinkish body, black and white tail. The two ladies are set on showing swaggering Falstaff the difference: the dove is gentle, the jay is brash and gaudy. More subtly, the two birds are being used to mean a faithful and beautiful lady and a made-up, immoral woman. Once again, Shakespeare takes conventional, literary birds and with the help of his keen observation turns them into vivid images.

CUCKOO AND HEDGE SPARROW

... Your cuckoo sings by kind.

— ALL'S WELL THAT ENDS WELL

'The plain-song cuckoo gray' of which Bottom sings in *A Midsummer Night's Dream* is a bird which has enjoyed a love-hate relationship with Man. Portia summed up one attitude in *The Merchant of Venice*:

> *He knows me as the blind man knows the cuckoo,*
> *By the bad voice.*

People dislike it – it has a dreadful but easily recognizable repetitive voice; I have heard of one which called 149 times non-stop! King Henry's description of his son, in the fine speech in *Henry IV, Part I* when he has a heart-to-heart talk about Hal's excesses, is even more solemn, also at the bird's expense:

> *So, when he had occasion to be seen,*
> *He was but as the cuckoo is in June,*
> *Heard, not regarded ...*

Curiously, this seems to be the only hint in Shakespeare of the many folk-lore rhymes which declare:

49

Cuckoo

> *In April come he shall;*
> *In May he sings all day;*
> *In June he changes his tune ...*

King Henry's cuckoo was not regarded because, as he says, 'a little more than a little is by much too much'. By June the cuckoo has almost stopped singing and hardly anyone is taking any notice of him. On the whole, however, the cuckoo's mention in folk-lore is more kindly, and much is connected with the bird's being a herald of spring like the swallow. Shakespeare reminds us of this and charmingly begs us to hear a dialogue in praise of the cuckoo in the final song of *Love's Labour's Lost.*

Although the cuckoo was welcomed as a harbinger of spring, it was also surrounded by much superstition, because it did not rear its own young. According to simple folk, it could sometimes be an omen. For example, in Norfolk and Sussex, if you were in bed when you heard the first cuckoo, that foretold illness or even death. People also believed that the cuckoo was foolish and, as today, applied the epithet to foolish people: Falstaff called Prince Hal in *Henry IV, Part I*: 'Ye cuckoo' and Bottom in *A Midsummer Night's Dream* asked:

> *... who would set his wit to so foolish a bird?*
> *Who would give a bird the lie, though he cry 'cuckoo' never so?*

Shakespeare's love of the country meant that he knew that 'the cuckoo builds not for himself'. What is more, he precisely described, more than once, a bird which is one of the most common substitute parents. One example occurs in *King Lear*:

> *For, you know, nuncle,*
> *The hedge-sparrow fed the cuckoo so long*
> *That it had its head bit off by its young.*

I doubt if a cuckoo has ever killed its foster-parent, but often the hedge-sparrow *appears* to lose its head, because its head is worn bald of feathers by repeated thrusting into the cuckoo's wide gape. (Although it looks superficially like a female house sparrow, this 'sparrow' is not at all related to the true sparrows and is referred to in modern bird-books by its old-English, provincial name of 'dunnock'.)

Cuckoo, Hedge-sparrow

OWL

We talk with goblins, owls, and sprites.

— COMEDY OF ERRORS

For thousands of years owls have fascinated people who hear them at night or see them in lonely places. Their big staring eyes and shrieks and hoots have inspired fear, even that fear of doom expressed by Lady Macbeth at the time of Duncan's murder:

> *It was the owl that shriek'd, the fatal bellman,*
> *Which gives the stern'st good-night.*

Indeed, even today, though we are so well-informed and sophisticated, a shiver goes down our spines when an owl hoots at midnight in a film or play. Then, the belief in the owl's ability to foretell death was so deep that even in the midst of comedy we find Puck singing in *A Midsummer Night's Dream* that

> *... the screetch-owl, screetching loud,*
> *Puts the wretch that lies in woe*
> *In remembrance of a shroud.*

In the seventeenth century this superstition was still widely believed by the common people while the educated were also familiar with it through the writings of classical authors.

53

Shakespeare combines folk belief with his Latin source in *Julius Caesar*:

> *And yesterday the bird of night did sit,*
> *Even at noon-day, upon the market-place,*
> *Hooting and shrieking.*

This bird was even more ominous because it was seen and heard at such an unusual time. Even today a birdwatcher gets excited if he sees an owl in daylight.

Curiously, that which causes terror can, by its very power, be used to drive it away. Many superstitious people in Europe and Asia believed that a dead owl nailed over the door kept evil away. The staring owl in *Love's Labour's Lost*

Barn Owl

with its 'merry note' is certainly not an evil bird. What is more, parts of an owl could be used medicinally; after all, there was a 'howlet's wing' in the cauldron in *Macbeth*!

Nowhere does Shakespeare use the specific name for an owl which you would find today in a bird book. But when Bolingbroke in *Henry VI, Part II* speaks of:

> *Deep night, dark night, the silent of the night . . .*
> *The time when screech owls cry . . .*

and when Lady Macbeth hears an owl *scream*, we can be sure that Shakespeare is thinking of the barn owl. The weird piercing scream. of the adult bird has made it known for centuries in Britain as the screech owl. What more ghostly

sight could there be to an impressionable eye than this white bird floating silently across the graveyard on its way to its brood in the church tower?

On the other hand, it is the tawny owl that Titania refers to in *A Midsummer Night's Dream* – 'the clamorous owl that nightly hoots,' – while the last song in *Love's Labour's Lost* perfectly records the traditional words which describe the tawny owl's call:

> *Then nightly sings the staring owl:*
> *'Tu-who;*
> *Tu-whit, tu-who' – A merry note . . .*

Another interesting reference to owls occurs in *Henry VI, Part III* when before the Battle of St Albans the Earl of Somerset says:

> *And he that will not fight for such a hope,*
> *Go home to bed and, like the owl by day,*
> *If he arise, be mock'd and wond'red at.*

Owls certainly *are* pestered and mobbed by small birds if they are found during daylight, which makes this comment the more telling.

LARK

...from the rising of the lark ...

— HENRY V

... I do hear the morning lark.

— A MIDSUMMER NIGHT'S DREAM

It would be difficult to find a bird more popular in literature than the lark. In Shakespeare's writings it occurs in at least fifteen plays and two poems. A fine song rarely gives a bird a prominent place in folk-lore. The lark's fine voice did, however, attract the attention of sensitive, poetic writers, who put it in the forefront of the popular birds of *literature*. It was also a bird well-known to country folk, and was first recorded in about the year 998 by Aelfric the Grammarian in his *Nomina Avium*. Shakespeare certainly knew it well. Its dull, streaky, earth-coloured plumage makes it hard to see and like several other birds, it would need an observant man to make sure he did not mistake 'this lark for a bunting' (*All's Well that Ends Well*).

The lark of which Shakespeare writes is the one whose full name is the skylark and which sings high in the sky. It appears, for example, in *King Lear*:

> *Look up a-height; the shrill-gorg'd lark so far*
> *Cannot be seen or heard.*

Skylark

Indeed, so high does it fly as it sings, that it is at 'heaven's gate' (*Cymbeline* and *Sonnet 29*).

Another feature of the skylark's song which appealed to Shakespeare was its singing so early in the morning. Time and again he remarks on it, each in a slightly different and original way: 'merry larks are ploughman's clocks' (*Love's Labour's Lost*) or 'Stir with the lark to-morrow, gentle Norfolk' (*Richard III*). The most famous reference occurs in *Romeo and Juliet*:

> *Wilt thou be gone? It is not yet near day;*
> *It was the nightingale, and not the lark,*
> *That pierc'd the fearful hollow of thine ear . . .*

58

Shakespeare was quick to use these attractive features of the lark – its song, and its early rising (we still say 'up with the lark') – in poetic images. Helena says of her friend Hermia, in *A Midsummer Night's Dream*:

> *Your eyes are lode-stars and your tongue's sweet air*
> *More tuneable than lark to shepherd's ear ...*

And he could not resist comparing larks with other birds: with the owl, to mark the difference between night and day, as when King Richard II cries, 'For night-owls shriek where mounting larks should sing'; with hawks, to emphasize the great height to which the birds could fly – 'hawks will soar Above the morning lark' (*The Taming of the Shrew*); and with the foreboding, evil raven, in the tragic and blood-thirsty tale *Titus Andronicus*, as when Titus receives news from the emperor that he can ransom his sons:

> *Did ever raven sing so like a lark*
> *That gives sweet tidings of the sun's uprise?*

59

HOUSE MARTIN

This guest of summer,
The temple-haunting martlet, does approve
By his lov'd mansionry that the heaven's breath
Smells wooingly here ...

— MACBETH

Banquo's careful description of the bird's *hanging* nest and the implication that there are many nests to be *seen* firmly support the identification of 'martlet' as the house martin. Martins build a wonderful cradle of mud which is plastered on to a wall or rock face, close under an overhang, so that there is an entrance hole left which is just big enough for the bird to enter. Further proof that Shakespeare was thinking of the house martin may be found in *The Merchant of Venice*. The Prince of Arragon, when deciding which casket to open, says that the foolish multitude chooses by show and outward appearances, and looks

> *... not to th' interior, but, like the martlet,*
> *Builds in the weather on the outward wall,*
> *Even in the force and road of casualty.*

Shakespeare has observed the nest so carefully, and has so clearly made the relatively tricky identification of the house martin, that it is rather surprising that he makes a character speak disparagingly of the bird's nest, which is a wonder of avian architecture. Martins' nests are usually so well sheltered from the elements beneath eaves or a rocky overhang that they are less in 'the force and road of casualty' than many woodland and hedgerow nests, which are in far greater danger from notorious egg-stealers such as magpies and jays.

I suppose to the layman it *does* seem less sensible to build a nest in the open; today we know that it is actually very sturdy. Recent studies have shown that it takes up to two weeks for both birds to build the nest from well over two thousand pellets of mud. Each pellet represents a beakful of mud, so they make more than two thousand journeys!

Banquo's comment as he stands before Macbeth's castle is more sympathetic and much nearer the truth:

> *... no jutty, frieze,*
> *Buttress, nor coign of vantage, but this bird*
> *Hath made her pendent bed and procreant cradle.*
> *Where they most breed and haunt, I have observ'd*
> *The air is delicate.*

These 'guests of summer' at a colony are delightful little migrants, darting black and white relatives of the much better known swallow, with purring flight calls which are an attractive feature of many an English farm and village.

ROBIN, WREN AND SWALLOW

Wren

. . . to relish a love-song, like a robin redbreast . . .
— TWO GENTLEMEN OF VERONA

The wren with little quill . . .
— A MIDSUMMER NIGHT'S DREAM

. . . daffodils,
That come before the swallow dares . . .
— THE WINTER'S TALE

Few birds have as much magical power and religious superstition connected with them as these three. In Britain, some
of the magical powers of the wren and robin are closely allied.
The robin has long been endowed with the power to look
after the dead, an idea associated with the superstition that
bad luck comes to him who harms or kills a robin. The well-
known nursery rhyme 'Who killed cock robin?' echoes this.

The wren was part of a cult which celebrated, shortly after Christmas, the defeat of dark winter and the coming of new light and life. Together with the swallow they had a reputation as the bringers of fire.

Although Shakespeare's scholarship, general knowledge and instinct to follow literary fashion led him to write of the legends associated with ravens, doves, eagles, owls and nightingales, he is curiously silent about the powers of these birds. The one exception is in *Cymbeline*. Arviragus carries in his sister, Imogen, believing her to be dead. In his lament he cries:

> *With fairest flowers,*
> *Whilst summer lasts and I live here, Fidele,*
> *I'll sweeten they sad grave ... the ruddock would,*
> *With charitable bill ... bring thee all this;*
> *Yea, and furr'd moss besides, when flow'rs are none,*
> *To winter-ground thy corse ...*

Robin

'Ruddock' was an old name for the robin; it is from an Anglo-Saxon word, and is clearly related to our adjective 'ruddy'. The belief that the robin covered the dead was widespread, and by the time Shakespeare wrote the play the story was already in print in T. Lupton's *A Thousand Notable Things* and Michael Drayton's *The Owle*. Drayton was a friend of Shakespeare and also came from Warwickshire. In more cheerful vein, Valentine's servant answers his master's question, 'Why, how know you that I am in love?' by saying '... you have learned ... to relish a love-song, like a robin redbreast' (*The Two Gentlemen of Verona*).

There are more references to wrens than to the other two birds put together. The wren's loud voice belies its small size, and the bird often brings attention to itself by sound not sight. The Earl of Suffolk has to tell King Henry VI of the death of his uncle; then he tries to comfort him, with little success, because the King angrily says:

> *What, doth my lord of Suffolk comfort me?*
> *Came he right now to sing a raven's note,*
> *Whose dismal tune bereft my vital powers;*
> *And thinks he that the chirping of a wren,*
> *By crying comfort from a hollow breast,*
> *Can chase away the first conceived sound?*

In no way was Suffolk's change of tune going to calm the King! King Henry's outburst is not typical of the high regard in which the wren's song has been held; in the seventeenth century it was sometimes kept as a song-bird in a cage.

64

Shakespeare does not often refer to birds' nesting habits. However, he knew that wrens sometimes reared large broods: 'Look where the youngest wren of nine comes,' says Sir Toby of Maria (*Twelfth Night*). Wrens usually lay five or six eggs, but more have been recorded on occasion, even as many as sixteen and eighteen.

Many Europeans look to the swallow as the first sign of summer. A dialogue in *Timon of Athens* recorded Shakespeare's awareness of the swallow's migratory habits:

TIMON. *And how fare you?*

FIRST LORD. *Ever at the best, hearing well of your Lordship.*

SECOND LORD. *The swallow follows not summer more willingly than we your Lordship.*

TIMON. [Aside] *Nor more willingly leaves winter; such summer-birds are men.*

Swallow

Timon's retort sounds very like the seventeenth century proverb, 'Swallows, like false friends, fly away upon the approach of winter.' In Shakespeare's day no-one knew for sure what happened to swallows in the winter; some believed they hibernated; others thought they flew south to warmer climes. The last, curious reference to the species occurs in *Antony and Cleopatra*:

> *Swallows have built*
> *In Cleopatra's sails their nests. The augurers*
> *Say they know not, they cannot tell; look grimly,*
> *And dare not speak their knowledge.*

Throughout Europe and Asia the swallows were a good omen; but if Cleopatra's ships had been so idle that the birds had built in the rigging, that certainly did not bode well for their seaworthiness!

Swallow

NIGHTINGALE

The nightingale, if she should sing by day,
When every goose is cackling, would be thought
No better a musician than the wren.

      — THE MERCHANT OF VENICE

By this, lamenting Philomel had ended
The well-tun'd warble of her nightly sorrow ...

      — THE RAPE OF LUCRECE

The rich brown colour of the nightingale is well hidden in the dense thickets, overgrown hedges and coppiced woodland which it loves. It is widespread in Europe, except the north, but in Britain it seems always to have been confined to an area south of a line between the Rivers Severn and Humber — which puts Warwickshire on the northern limit of its range.

However, there is no doubt that even if Shakespeare did not hear one at home, he must have heard either a wild one somewhere in south-east England, where it is a common summer visitor, or a caged one ('twenty caged nightingales' were offered to Christopher Sly in *The Taming of the Shrew*).

The name 'nightingale' comes from the Old English words for 'night' and 'to sing'. Most bird books today describe it as a magnificent singer during both day and night, but specially fond of dusk and the early hours of the night when its rich and varied song is not competing with other songsters. It is very likely that Europeans have called it the 'night-singer' because its song is most noticeable then, filling still early summer evenings for hours on end. So it is not surprising that Shakespeare puts the above words into Portia's mouth, although most birdwatchers today would disagree with her!

In ancient Greek mythology, as recorded by Ovid, Tereus cut out Philomel's tongue, but the Gods took pity on her and turned her into a nightingale; presumably Shakespeare's learning in the classics gave rise to his allowing Aaron, 'that damn'd Moor,' to say: 'His Philomel must lose her tongue today ...' as he plots against Bassianus and his loved-one Lavinia in *Titus Andronicus*.

Even more curious is another literary conceit used by Shakespeare and his contemporaries, one of whom, Thomas Lodge, introduced it into English literature. Fancifully it describes the nightingale singing sadly as it presses its breast against a thorn and is found in *The Rape of Lucrece*:

Come, Philomel, that sing'st of ravishment ...
And whiles against a thorn thou bear'st thy part
To keep thy sharp woes waking ...

It is not clear how such a strange belief came about, but the authority on bird folk-lore, the Rev. E. Armstrong, says it most probably came into English literature from Persian poetry via French literature!

Shakespeare seems to have been in two minds about this bird. As an observant countryman he had heard the nightingale's 'well-tuned warble'. But as a poet, steeped in poetic tradition, he wrote of 'her nightly sorrow'. Indeed, this divided loyalty shows very clearly in his work: the poems and songs invariably capture *Philomel's* lament 'that sings of ravishment'; but the plays tell of the English *nightingale* singing in natural woodland. For example, Valentine, one of the *Two Gentlemen of Verona*, after he has been banished, soliloquizes:

This shadowy desert, unfrequented woods,
I better brook than flourishing peopled towns.
Here can I sit alone, unseen of any,
And to the nightingale's complaining notes
Tune my distresses and record my woes.

It has been very rare for any bird to be given the status in a nation's literature that poets have given to the nightingale. So it is particularly striking when we find Shakespeare letting his feelings as a countryman overcome his poetic instincts. In

69

Sonnet 102 he clearly shows his knowledge of the bird's short period of song, which lasts only from the end of April to early June:

> *As Philomel in summer's front doth sing,*
> *And stops her pipe in growth of riper days ...*

And in *A Midsummer Night's Dream* the magic created by the nightingale's wonderful song breaks through the sorrow of which classical legends say the bird is supposed to sing:

> *Philomel with melody*
> *Sing in our sweet lullaby.*
> *Lulla, lulla, lullaby; lulla, lulla, lullaby.*
> *Never harm*
> *Nor spell nor charm*
> *Come our lovely lady nigh.*
> *So good night, with lullaby.*

Blackbird and Starlings

BLACKBIRD, THRUSH AND STARLING

Jay and Song Thrush

With heigh! with heigh! the thrush and the jay ...
— THE WINTER'S TALE

Many people today who are not birdwatchers will say that they can recognize a blackbird and a thrush, but they would get stuck telling a cock blackbird from a starling, and a song thrush from a mistle thrush. Although they are all very common birds, they are not mentioned much in literature.

It is surprising that the blackbird, in particular, hardly features in our folklore, despite being a bird conspicuous for both its appearance and strikingly attractive song. Over the years two names for the bird have fought for supremacy: although 'blackbird' is first recorded in literature in *The Book of St Albans* of 1486, the northern half of Britain favoured 'ouzel' or 'ousel' (which still survives in the name of the blackbird's relative, the ring ouzel). It is the second name which Shakespeare uses twice. In *Henry IV, Part II* Justice Silence tells Justice Shallow that his daughter is 'Alas, a black ousel' – a shame that such a lovely species should be used to describe a girl whose hair is unfashionably black. But Shakespeare really knew his blackbird as a fine bird of woodland glades, for he makes Bottom in *A Midsummer Night's Dream* sing of

> *The ousel cock, so black of hue,*
> *With orange-tawny bill . . .*

That's a perfect description of the bird! In the same song Bottom sings of 'The throstle with his note so true', and Portia in *The Merchant of Venice*, describing one of her suitors, says that 'if a throstle sing', the French lord immediately starts dancing! The song thrush is the species referred to; 'throstle' was the common name for it in literature from Chaucer onwards, and it was a name used until recently in some northern counties of England. Its pure, flute-like notes and habit of repeating perfectly a song-phrase clearly show that it was the song thrush that sang with 'note so true'. One is tempted to say that Autolycus in *The Winter's Tale* was singing of the same species, because the repeated 'With heigh! With heigh!' echoes the song thrush's song. But, tantalizingly, the word 'thrush' on its own was used by William Turner in his *Avium Praecipuarum Historia* to mean the *mistle* thrush. (If Shakespeare knew a bird book, it would have been this one.) Now, although it may be the birds' song which 'Doth set [his] pugging tooth on edge', Autolycus also seems to thoroughly enjoy the sound. Was Shakespeare having fun? Song thrushes were reared from chicks because they made fine singing cage-birds, but the wild, far less tuneful song of the *mistle* thrush might be attractive only to 'a snapper-up of unconsidered trifles' like Autolycus.

Blackbird

The apparent similarity of the starling and the blackbird led to their being classed in Shakespeare's time as close relatives, although today we know they are members of very different families. Shakespeare *did* know one striking fact about the starling which is still true today – it is an excellent mimic. I have heard it imitate the curlew, blue tit, blackbird and a boy's 'wolf-whistle'. Hotspur in *Henry IV, Part I*, in order 'to gall and pinch this Bolingbroke', had a bright idea:

> *But I will find him when he lies asleep,*
> *And in his ear I'll holla 'Mortimer!'*
> *Nay,*
> *I'll have a starling shall be taught to speak*
> *Nothing but 'Mortimer', and give it him*
> *To keep his anger still in motion.*

The starling was noted in the seventeenth century for imitating a man's voice and for speaking clearly.

Starling

ROOK, MAGPIE, JACKDAW, CHOUGH AND JAY

The crows and choughs that wing the midway air ...
— KING LEAR

And chattering pies in dismal discords sung ...
— HENRY VI, PART III

Birdwatchers will often confess to having a favourite bird. Some have observed one so carefully that they have written a book about it; others have concentrated on a whole family. The five birds named above, together with the raven and the crow, represent all the members of the crow family in Britain. It is fascinating to wonder why Shakespeare wrote about this family especially.

'Scare*crows*' (see p.84) were used to keep *rooks* away from the grain ('crow' was often used in former times for 'rook'). Shakespeare well knew the subtle differences between the two birds; the lazy eye sees all big black birds as 'crows'. Macbeth's mind, 'full of scorpions' is confused as he notices that 'the crow makes wing to the rooky wood'. Is it a lone rook, last back to the rookery to roost? That would be a good omen, for it was believed that ill would befall anyone near a

75

rookery deserted by the birds. Or is it really a crow, a bird of bad luck, a final daytime misery before 'night's black agent's come forth? Soon afterwards, Macbeth sees the Ghost of Banquo and then declares:

> *It will have blood; they say blood will have blood.*
> *Stones have been known to move and trees to speak;*
> *Augurs and understood relations have*
> *By maggot-pies and choughs and rooks brought forth*
> *The secret'st man of blood.*

Rooks

His misery is complete. The magpie has long been a bird of superstition, with rhymes throughout the British Isles giving variations on a theme:

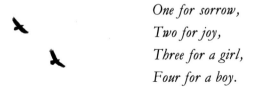

> *One for sorrow,*
> *Two for joy,*
> *Three for a girl,*
> *Four for a boy.*

The name 'magpie' is a shortened form of 'maggot-pie' (from the French 'Margot', a diminutive of 'Marguerite' — its chattering was supposed to resemble a talkative woman). In this story of death there may be a pun on 'maggot'. Macbeth may also be thinking of the bad luck supposed to come from seeing either *one* magpie ('One for sorrow') or seven magpies ('Seven for the devil' occurs in a Scottish version of the same folk-rhyme and Macbeth was a Scot).

Magpies

Choughs and Jackdaws

Macbeth's reference to 'chough' is interesting too. This name was often given to the jackdaw, and that small crow, with its steely-blue eyes and grey nape, was certainly meant in Puck's 'russet-pated choughs'. In Shakespeare's time 'russet' could mean 'grey' as well as 'reddish-brown'. The birds were also called simply 'daws', a name used by Iago in *Othello*. 'Jackdaw' did not become popular until well after Shakespeare's time. In *King Lear*, Edgar tells Gloucester as they stand on a hill near Dover that 'The crows and choughs that wing the midway air show scarce so gross as beetles' as they fly below them. It is possible that chough here refers to the Cornish chough, which years ago used to breed on the Dover cliffs. Jackdaws like their own company; their constant chatter is a feature of many a cliff or ruin, and this must have been in mind when Shakespeare made a Lord in *All's Well That Ends Well* say that he and a soldier must speak 'choughs' language, gabble enough, and good enough'.

In contrast, the loveliest of the crow family is the jay, which is nothing like its relatives in colour. Autolycus sings of it, together with the lark and the thrush. It is curious to put it with these song birds, because the jay's voice is a dreadful squawk – just like the rogue's? Shakespeare was well aware

of its striking colour; Petruchio remarks on it in an angry exchange with Katherine in *The Taming of the Shrew*:

> *What, if the jay more precious than the lark*
> *Because his feathers are more beautiful?*

One of Shakespeare's rare references to a bird's nest is in Caliban's promise to Trinculo to show him a jay's nest (*The Tempest*). This nest is far and away the hardest crow's nest to find. Perhaps Shakespeare had found such a nest when he was a boy and remembered the achievement in Caliban's wish to show Trinculo something special.

Jay

RAVEN AND CARRION CROW

... ravens, crows, and kites,
Fly o'er our heads ...

— JULIUS CAESAR

Since ancient times the raven has played a prominent part in religion, superstition and legend. Across much of Europe, Asia and North America it figures in oral tradition, pictures and artifacts as the Bird of Doom or the Bird of the Flood.

The raven is the largest crow: all black, two feet long and with a four-foot wing-span. In wild places, its size, deep call and love of carrion strike terror into man. Because it was so often found near the dead – animals or men on a battlefield – it was considered able to foretell death, as Lady Macbeth implied in her speech when she knew the King was coming:

> *The raven himself is hoarse*
> *That croaks the fatal entrance of Duncan*
> *Under my battlements.*

And Thersites, in *Troilus and Cressida*, wishes he could 'croak like a raven'; in that case he 'would bode'.

In *Titus Andronicus* Tamora speaks of the 'fatal raven', but later Lavinia says that 'some say that ravens foster forlorn children'. The *helpful* ravens are in the Christian tradition which reversed the pagan one and had scriptural authority in God's providing food for the ravens and their feeding Elijah (see 1 Kings 17 and Psalm 147).

Shakespeare was too observant a countryman to name the raven only in conventional, literary ways. In *Sonnet 127* he fascinatingly mixes the idea from 'the old age' that 'black was not counted fair' with his own thrill that 'now is black beauty's successive heir' and that his 'mistress' brows are raven black'. Even Thersites' onomatopaeic 'I would croak like a raven' has a real-life sound as well as malevolent overtones. Shakespeare had almost certainly heard one, although

today the species is rarely seen in the eastern half of Britain.

The crow looks very like a raven, and has taken on some of that bird's evil – at Philippi, for example, as we are told in *Julius Caesar*. Elsewhere, in *A Midsummer Night's Dream*, Titania harangues Oberon and describes the present time, saying that:

> *The fold stands empty in the drowned field,*
> *And crows are fatted on the murrain flock . . .*

('murrain' means 'dead of disease'). This surely describes what Shakespeare had seen, and makes the literary crows into real carrion crows. These common birds gave Shakespeare

many good ideas for rich descriptions. Belarius tells the young sons of Cymbeline to climb the hills to hunt for venison; he will remain below and 'you above perceive me like a crow', from a great distance. When Portia and Nerissa return home from the trial in *The Merchant of Venice*, Nerissa admires the music but Portia says:

> *The crow doth sing as sweetly as the lark*
> *When neither is attended . . .*

She continues this melancholy train of thought, naming four other birds within ten more lines. In *The Winter's Tale* Autolycus sings of 'Cypress black as e'er was crow', and in the glorious muddle of twins in *The Comedy of Errors* we find Antipholus and Dromio of Ephesus having bother with 'A crow without a feather' and 'an iron crow': in other words, a crowbar!

Several times Shakespeare effectively compares the black grimness of a crow with a prettier bird, as when Benvolio in *Romeo and Juliet* says he can show Romeo a more attractive girlfriend than Rosaline:

> *Compare her face with some that I shall show,*
> *And I will make thee think thy swan a crow.*

In the same play, Benvolio speaks of 'scaring the ladies like a crow-keeper'; King Lear speaks of a fellow that looks 'like a crow-keeper'. Both men mean a person who scares the crows off a corn field, a scarecrow. It seems likely that the name 'crow' is here being used for 'rook', which is

84

very similar to look at but feeds on grain fields in flocks, unlike 'the knavish crows ... all impatient for their hour' (*Henry V*), which are more interested in carrion. Many of us have seen a scarecrow which has been so long in the same place in a field that the birds are no longer scared, and even use it as a perch. It is delightful to record that Shakespeare had seen the same, and worked it into a fine metaphor in *Measure for Measure*:

> *We must not make a scarecrow of the law,*
> *Setting it up to fear the birds of prey,*
> *And let it keep one shape till custom make it*
> *Their perch, and not their terror.*

Buzzard

SPARROW, FINCH, BUNTING AND WAGTAIL

Yellowhammer and Chaffinch

... She fetches her breath as short as a new-ta'en sparrow.

TROILUS AND CRESSIDA

Sparrows have probably always been common in England since man first provided ample nest-sites in his own dwellings. They have never been favourite birds; their monotonous chirping, dull plumage and habit of grubbing in back yards have not endeared them to many people, least of all to Angelo in *Measure for Measure*, of whom Lucio says: 'Sparrows must not build in his house-eaves because they are lecherous.' In *Troilus and Cressida*, Thersites has a poor opinion of sparrows too; he is angry with Ajax and amongst other things grumbles: 'I will buy nine sparrows for a penny, and his pia mater is not worth the ninth part of a sparrow.'

House Sparrows

But Shakespeare does not consistently undervalue the bird, because he twice echoes the words of Jesus: 'Are not sparrows two a penny? Yet without your Father's leave not one of them can fall to the ground' (Matthew 10.29). Firstly, Oliver's servant, Adam, in *As You Like It* prays:

> *... He that doth the ravens feed,*
> *Yea, providently caters for the sparrow,*
> *Be comfort to my age!*

Secondly, Hamlet rather fatalistically says to Horatio just before the final duel, 'There is a special providence in the fall of a sparrow'.

Three other small birds are mentioned by Shakespeare. All are very attractive; they would be well-known to an observant countryman, especially one such as Shakespeare who often travelled the country roads between Stratford and London. Bottom sings in *A Midsummer Night's Dream* of 'the finch' – we are told no more, though we can guess that he meant the chaffinch, for as Willughby wrote of it in 1678, 'Neither is there any bird more frequent in all parts of this land excepting perchance the Lark, the Sparrow and the Yellowhammer.' Modern studies have shown it to be one of *our* commonest birds, too. I wonder if Lafeu's 'I took this lark for a bunting' (*All's Well That Ends Well*) refers to the yellowhammer, which is a kind of bunting. A female *would*

88

look superficially like a lark and at times they forage together on stubble. Lastly, Kent's angry cry, 'Spare my grey beard, you wagtail?' (*King Lear*) accurately describes poor, nervous Oswald, who must be too scared to stand still and is bowing obsequiously, bobbing up and down as repeatedly as a pied wagtail moves its tail.

Now, at the end, we can look back and feel that we can say with Shakespeare and the exiled Duke in *As You Like It*:

> *And this our life, exempt from public haunt,*
> *Finds tongues in trees, books in the running brooks,*
> *Sermons in stones, and good in everything.*
> *I would not change it.*

Pied Wagtail

Suggestions for Further Reading

ALEXANDER, MARGUERITE. *Shakespeare and His Contemporaries* (Pan, London, 1979).

ARMSTRONG, EDWARD A. *Shakespeare's Imagination: a study of the psychology of association and inspiration* (Lindsay Drummond, London, 1946).

ARMSTRONG, EDWARD A. *The Folklore of Birds* (Collins, London, 1958).

BURGESS, ANTHONY. *Shakespeare* (Penguin, Harmondsworth, 1972).

DENT, ALAN. *World of Shakespeare: Sports and Pastimes* (Osprey, Reading, 1973).

DODD, A.H. *Elizabethan England* (Batsford, London, 1974).

FISHER, JAMES. *A History of Birds* (Hutchinson, London, 1954).

FORD, BORIS (ed.). *The Age of Shakespeare* (Penguin, Harmondsworth, 1955).

FOX, LEVI. *An Illustrated Introduction to Shakespeare's Birds* (Jarrold, Norwich, 1977).

GEIKIE, SIR A. *The Birds of Shakespeare* (J. Maclehose & Sons, Glasgow, 1916).

HARTING, J.E. *The Ornithology of Shakespeare critically examined, explained and illustrated* (London, 1871).

HAYMAN, PETER. *The Birdwatcher's Pocket Guide* (Mitchell Beazley, London 1979).

HOGG, GARRY. *The Colour Book of Shakespeare's Country* (Batsford, London 1976).

PETERSON, R.T., et al., *A Field Guide to the Birds of Britain and Europe* (Collins, London, 3rd edn. 1974).

RAY, JOHN. *The Ornithology of Francis Willughby* (1678). Facsimile limited reprint, Paul Minet, Newport Pagnall, 1972).

SHARROCK, J.T.R. (ed.), *The Atlas of the Breeding Birds of Britain and Ireland* (B.T.O./I.W.C., Tring, 1976).

SWANN, H. KIRKE. *A Dictionary of English and Folk Names of British Birds* (Witherby, London, 1913).

WILSON, JOHN DOVER. *Life in Shakespeare's England* (Penguin, Harmondsworth, 1964).

90

Index of Birds

(Italic numbers indicate illustrations,
arabic numbers indicate text)

Barnacle Goose, 13, 20, *21, 22, 23*
Barn Owl, *54*, 55
Blackbird, *70*, 71, 72 *73*, 74
Bunting, 88
Buzzard, 36, *39, 85*

Carrion Crow, 75, 76, 83–85
Chaffinch, *86*, 88
Chough, *78*, 79
Cormorant, 13, 18, *19*
Crow, *see* Carrion Crow
Cuckoo, 49, *50–52*

Dabchick, *18*
Diver, *see* Great Northern Diver
Dove, *see* Turtle Dove
Duck, 13
Duck Hawk, *see* Peregrine Falcon
Dunnock, *see* Hedge Sparrow

Eagle, 33–35, *see also* Golden Eagle

Falcon, *see* Peregrine Falcon
Finch, *see* Chaffinch

Golden Eagle, *34*
Goose, *see* Barnacle Goose
Goshawk, 28

Great Northern Diver, 14
Grebe, 18, *see also* Dabchick
Gull, 14, 15

Hawk, 15, 29, 30, 32
Hedge Sparrow, 49, *52*
Heron, *14*, 15, 16
House Martin, 60, 61

Jackdaw, *78, 79*
Jay, 48, *71*, 79, *80*

Kestrel, 32
Kingfisher, *15*, 16, *17*
Kite, *see* Red Kite

Lapwing, 42, *43*, 45
Lark, *see* Skylark

Magpie, *77*
Mallard, *see* Duck
Martin, *see* House Martin
Mistle Thrush, 73

Nightingale, *67*, 68–70

Osprey, 36, 37
Ousel Cock, *see* Blackbird

Owl, 53–56, *see also* Barn Owl, Tawny Owl

Partridge, 40, 41
Peregrine Falcon, 9, *14, 27*, 28, *30*
Pheasant, 40, 41
Pied Wagtail, *89*
Pigeon, 47
Puttock, *see* Red Kite

Quail, 40

Raven, *35*, 59, 81, 82
Red Kite, 8, *35*, 36, 37, *38*, 39
Robin, 62, *63*, 64
Rook, 8, 75, *76*

Skylark, 8, 57, *58*, 59, *88*
Snipe, *43*, 44

Song Thrush, *6, 71*, 72, 73
Sparrow, 86, *87, see also* Hedge Sparrow
Staniel, *see* Kestrel
Starling, *70, 74*
Swallow, 62, 63, *65, 66*
Swan, *10*, 11, 12

Tawny Owl, 56
Thrush, 73, *see also* Song Thrush, Mistle
    Thrush
Turtle Dove, *46, 47*, 48

Wagtail, *see* Pied Wagtail
Woodcock, 25, 26, 42, *43*, 44, 45
Wren, *62*, 63–65

Yellowhammer, *86, 88*

Index of Shakespearean Sources

The quotations follow the text of *The Tudor Shakespeare*,
Ed. Peter Alexander (Collins, 1951).

PAGE

9   Titus Andronicus, II.iii
The Rape of Lucrece, line 511
As You Like It, V.iii

10   Henry VI, Part I, V.iii
Titus Andronicus, IV.ii

11   Othello, V.ii

12   Cymbeline, III.iv
The Rape of Lucrece, lines 1008–12

13   Richard II, II.i
Antony and Cleopatra, III.x

14   Macbeth, V.iii
Timon of Athens, II.i

15   Hamlet, II.ii

16   Henry VI, Part II.ii
King Lear, II.ii

18   Venus and Adonis, lines 86–87

19   Troilus and Cressida, II.ii
Love's Labour's Lost, I.i
Coriolanus, I.i

20   The Tempest, IV.i

24   The Merry Wives of Windsor, III.iii
A Midsummer Night's Dream, III.ii
The Tempest, II.i

25   Venus and Adonis, line 67

26   Hamlet, I.iii and V.ii
Henry VI, Part III, I.iv
Henry VI, Part II, I.iii; II.iv; III.iii
Much Ado About Nothing, III.i

26   Twelfth Night, III.iv

27   Romeo and Juliet, II.ii
Hamlet, I.v

28   Troilus and Cressida, III.ii
Henry VI, Part II, II.i

29   The Taming of the Shrew, IV.i

30   Othello, III.iii

31   The Taming of the Shrew, I.i
Twelfth Night, II.v

32   The Merry Wives of Windsor, III.iii
Macbeth, II.iii

33   Cymbeline, IV.ii
Romeo and Juliet, III.v
Richard II,III.iii

34   Richard III, I.i
Titus Andronicus, IV.iv

35   Julius Caesar, V.i

36   The Taming of the Shrew, II.i
King Lear, I.iv
Coriolanus, IV.vii

37   Cymbeline, I.i
Henry VI, Part II, III.ii
Troilus and Cressida, V.i

38   Henry VI, Part II, V.ii

39   The Winter's Tale, IV.iii
The Taming of the Shrew, II.i

40   Antony and Cleopatra, II.iii
Much Ado About Nothing, II.i

93

PAGE

41 The Winter's Tale, IV.iv
42 Measure for Measure, I.iv
   Much Ado About Nothing, V.i
   Othello, I.iii
   The Taming of the Shrew, I.ii
44 Love's Labour's Lost, IV.iii
   Hamlet, I.iii
45 Hamlet, V.ii
   Measure for Measure, I.iv
   Much Ado About Nothing, III.i
   The Comedy of Errors, IV.ii
46 A Midsummer Night's Dream, I.ii
47 The Merchant of Venice, II.ii
   Venus and Adonis, line 153
   As You Like It, I.ii
48 King Lear, IV.iv
   Troilus and Cressida, III.ii
   The Merry Wives of Windsor, III.iii
49 All's Well That Ends Well, I.iii
   A Midsummer Night's Dream, III.i
   The Merchant of Venice, V.i
   Henry IV, Part I, III.ii
50 Love's Labour's Lost, V.ii
51 Henry IV, Part I, II.iv
   A Midsummer Night's Dream, III.i
52 King Lear, I.iv
53 The Comedy of Errors, II.ii
   Macbeth, II.ii
   A Midsummer Night's Dream, V.i
54 Julius Caesar, I.iii
   Love's Labour's Lost, V.ii
55 Macbeth, IV.i
   Henry VI, Part II, I.iv
   Macbeth, II.ii
56 A Midsummer Night's Dream, II.ii
   Love's Labour's Lost, V.ii

PAGE

56 Henry VI, Part III, V.iv
57 Henry V, III.vii
   A Midsummer Night's Dream, IV.i
   All's Well That Ends Well, II.v
   King Lear, IV.vi
58 Cymbeline, II.iii
   Sonnet 29
   Love's Labour's Lost, V.ii
   Richard III, V.iii
   Romeo and Juliet, III.v
59 A Midsummer Night's Dream, I.i
   Richard II, III.iii
   The Taming of the Shrew, The Induction, 2
   Titus Andronicus, III.i
60 Macbeth, I.vi
   The Merchant of Venice, II.ix
61 Macbeth, I.vi
62 The Two Gentlemen of Verona, II.i
   A Midsummer Night's Dream, III.i
   The Winter's Tale, IV.iv
63 Cymbeline, IV.ii
64 The Two Gentlemen of Verona, II.i
   Henry VI, Part II, III.ii
65 Twelfth Night, III.ii
   Timon of Athens, III.vi
66 Antony and Cleopatra, IV.xii
67 The Merchant of Venice, V.i
   The Rape of Lucrece, lines 1079–80
68 The Taming of the Shrew, The Induction,
   Titus Andronicus, II.iii
   The Rape of Lucrece, lines 1128 and 1135–
69 The Two Gentlemen of Verona, V.iv
70 Sonnet 102
70 A Midsummer Night's Dream, II.ii
71 The Winter's Tale, IV.iii
72 Henry IV, Part II, III.ii

94

PAGE

72 A Midsummer Night's Dream, III.i
   The Merchant of Venice, I.ii
73 The Winter's Tale, IV.iii
74 Henry IV, Part I, I.iii
75 King Lear, IV.vi
   Henry VI, Part III, V.vi
75 Macbeth, III.ii
76 Macbeth, III.iv
78 A Midsummer Night's Dream, III.ii
   Othello, I.i
   King Lear, IV.vi
79 All's Well That Ends Well, IV.i
80 The Taming of the Shrew, IV.iii
   The Tempest, II.ii
81 Julius Caesar, V.i
   Macbeth, I.v
   Troilus and Cressida, V.ii
   Titus Andronicus, II.iii
82 Sonnet 127
83 Julius Caesar, V.i

PAGE

83 A Midsummer Night's Dream, II.i
84 Cymbeline, III.iii
   The Merchant of Venice, V.i
   The Winter's Tale, IV.iv
   The Comedy of Errors, III.i
   Romeo and Juliet, I.ii
   Romeo and Juliet, I.iv
   King Lear, IV.vi
85 Henry V, IV.ii
   Measure for Measure, II.i
86 Troilus and Cressida, III.ii
   Measure for Measure, III.ii
   Troilus and Cressida, II.i
87 As You Like It, II.iii
   Hamlet, V.ii
88 A Midsummer Night's Dream, III.i
   All's Well That Ends Well, II.v
89 King Lear, II.ii
   As You Like It, II.i

Index of Plays and Poems

All's Well That Ends Well, 49, 57, 79, 88

Antony and Cleopatra, 13, 40, 66

As You Like It, 9, 47, 87, 89

The Comedy of Errors, 45, 53, 83

Coriolanus, 19, 36

Cymbeline, 12, 33, 37, 58, 63, 84

Hamlet, 15, 26, 27, 44, 45, 87

Henry IV, Part I, 49, 51, 74

Henry IV, Part II, 72

Henry V, 57, 85

Henry VI, Part I, 10, 16

Henry VI, Part II, 26, 28, 37, 38, 55, 64

Henry VI, Part III, 26, 56, 75

Julius Caesar, 35, 54, 81, 83

King Lear, 16, 36, 48, 52, 57, 75, 78, 83, 89

Love's Labour's Lost, 19, 44, 50, 54, 56, 58

Macbeth, 14, 32, 53, 55, 60, 61, 75, 76, 81

Measure for Measure, 42, 45, 85, 86

The Merchant of Venice, 47, 49, 60, 67, 72, 83

The Merry Wives of Windsor, 24, 32, 48

A Midsummer Night's Dream, 24, 46, 49, 51, 53, 56, 57, 59, 62, 70, 72, 78, 83, 88

Much Ado About Nothing, 26, 40, 42, 45

Othello, 11, 30, 42, 78

The Rape of Lucrece, 9, 12, 67, 68

Richard II, 13, 33, 59

Richard III, 34, 58

Romeo and Juliet, 27, 33, 58, 83

Sonnets, 58, 70, 82

The Taming of the Shrew, 29, 31, 36, 39, 42, 59, 68, 80

The Tempest, 20, 24, 80

Timon of Athens, 14, 65

Titus Andronicus, 9, 10, 34, 59, 68, 81

Troilus and Cressida, 19, 28, 37, 48, 81, 86

Twelfth Night, 26, 31, 65

The Two Gentlemen of Verona, 62, 64, 68

Venus and Adonis, 18, 25, 47

The Winter's Tale, 39, 41, 62, 71, 73, 83